# Fl                                        re:
## 16 Project                          o Treasure

DISCARD

DISCARD

DEMCO

# *F*lea Market *F*urniture

**16 Projects**

*to Turn Trash to Treasure*

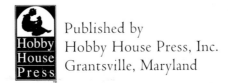

Published by
Hobby House Press, Inc.
Grantsville, Maryland

Additional copies of this book may be purchased at $22.95
(plus postage and handling) from
**Hobby House Press, Inc.**
1 Corporate Drive, Grantsville, MD 21536
1-800-554-1447
www.hobbyhouse.com or from your favorite bookstore or dealer.

Printed in the United States of America

ISBN: 0-87588-664-7

R03028 82079

# Dedication

This book is dedicated to my children, Gabriella and Ian—my best projects and the source of endless creativity.

# Acknowledgements

I'd like to thank everyone who helped me put this book together especially the production team at Hobby House Press, Inc. I'd also like to thank my husband for helping me with the projects and for letting me use his tools. Thanks to my mother who babysat on countless occasions so that I could work on my book or attend various flea markets in search of the next project. And thanks to my grandmother for always letting me go treasure hunting in her attic.

# Table of Contents

# Introduction

What used to be grandpa's Saturday ritual has become a national craze. And why not? Where else can you get so much for so little? Anyone can find a bargain and turn it into something special.

My intention with this book is to show you how to get the shabby chic look on a budget by giving new life to inexpensive second-hand furniture. Being a new first-time home owner, I can relate to decorating dilemmas faced when trying to furnish a house. I also hope that it inspires you to find unusual ways to make something out of nothing. You don't have to be a designer to be creative and to reinvent furniture to meet your needs; you just need a little guidance. That's what I hope to achieve in this book.

This full-color handbook contains simple do-it-yourself techniques to show you how to transform inexpensive castoffs into attractive pieces for your home. I encourage you to look past the wobbly legs, terrible paint jobs, and faded fabrics and think about what each piece of junk can become. First, we begin with the basic tools and techniques that you need to do most any project. I've tried to give you methods that require as few power tools as possible, but sometimes it's next to impossible to avoid and sometimes it just doesn't make sense to do things by hand. If you find that I've used power tools that you don't have, check with your local home center to see if they rent out tools to do-it-yourselfers.

After covering basic tools and techniques, we look at 16 projects from beginning to end transforming even the most unsightly furniture into spectacular additions to your home. From minor fixes to complete overhauls, this book addresses all levels of skill, and hopefully gives you some inspiring ideas for your own furniture fix-ups.

# The Quest

## Where to Look

I can remember when it was somewhat taboo to admit that you picked something up at a yard sale or rummage sale, but times have changed. What once was a well-kept secret of interior designers and antiques dealers has become a national trend— shopping the flea market. Not only is it thrifty, but it's fun! You can find terrific one-of-a-kind items at bargain prices as well as find new and unexpected uses for ordinary objects. This leads to a decorating style that is uniquely yours and infinitely creative.

The quest to find great items and great bargains has admittedly become more challenging as more people flock to flea markets that have somehow been taken over by odd mixes of antiques and collectibles along with T-shirts and craft items. However, the treasures are there for the taking if you're willing to search them out.

Flea markets are typically wonderful places to hunt for treasures as the variety of items can be overwhelming at times, but don't overlook other places to find one-of-a-kind items or that last plate to complete your collection. Yard sales, especially town-wide yard sales, can also be promising places to find bargains. Also, don't forget to check the newspaper for estate auctions though you will need to be careful not to get caught up in the excitement of bidding or your bargain will quickly become a priceless heirloom. Thrift shops can harbor some fantastic items that are worth browsing through as these shops handle such vast quantities of items that they rarely know the value of many items. Finally, don't overlook antique shops and antique fairs. Generally these are least likely to produce a bargain as the merchandise is typically in better shape and are priced higher, but it's still fun to peruse the isles.

## What to Wear

If you've ever been to an outdoor flea market, you know that you have to contend with the environment. Be it dust from passing vehicles or mud from last night's rain shower, you will want to wear clothes and shoes that you don't mind getting a little dingy. You will probably want to dress in layers as well since many times a chilly morning will turn into a blazingly hot summer day. Don't forget to include sunscreen as part of your attire and even a hat of some sort. In addition, you may be walking for hours, so be sure that your shoes fit well and are comfortable. There's nothing like sore feet to cut the day short.

## What to Bring

Cash. Some dealers will take a personal check, but generally it's cash only. And forget about the credit cards when attending flea markets and yard sales. No one accepts them and you run the risk of losing them so it's best just to leave them at home. Lots of single bills and nothing higher than $20 bills is helpful.

You want to carry as little as possible so make sure that you only bring the essentials. If you just can't leave home without the kitchen sink, put it in a backpack and wear it properly balancing the weight on both shoulders, not just one. Still, a large load will eventually cause your back to ache and will turn your fun day into a literal "pain in the neck."

Old grocery bags are handy if a vendor runs out. They are also easy to jam into a small pack.

Finally, bring something to drink—water preferably. Long days in the hot sun can mean dehydration and heat exhaustion. Often you can find drinks for sale, but why buy a soda when you can bring your water bottle along for free?

## Bargaining Etiquette

Vendors may act insulted if you try to bargain for a better price, but most expect it. However, there are some basic rules to follow. First and foremost, don't be afraid to try—if you don't try, you'll never know if you could have gotten an even better deal. Second, you generally don't want to bargain for a price that is more than 30% off of the ticketed price. Anything less than that will most certainly annoy the dealer. For instance, if you see an item for $100, you generally don't want to ask the dealer if he or she will take anything less than $70. A dealer is likely to meet you half way on an item. Third, practice your poker face. Even if your heart is pounding with excitement, your actions should suggest that you could take it or leave it. Finally, if you do strike a deal with the seller, be prepared to make good on it right then and there. Don't come to an agreement only to tell him that you will be back after you finish shopping or, in other words, when you make sure there's nothing better. That's just rude and he or she has no reason to hold the item in case you come back.

# To Save or Not to Save

## Antique vs Junk

In this book we are talking about junk furniture that is generally unwanted because it is ugly, broken, battered or just plain old. We are not talking about antiques that will lose their value if you touch the finish no matter how far gone they are. Remember, once you've altered an item's finish, it can never be "original" again so make certain that you truly want to refinish something before altering what may seem like a worthless piece of junk when it is really an antique. The items in this book are most definitely unwanted in their current condition—neglected items with little or no value if not otherwise repaired or refinished.

You will need to practice seeing past the unsightly exteriors and envision what such pieces of furniture can become given some creativity and tender loving care. But don't become so enamored that you can't see the real problems. The excitement of buying a bargain piece of furniture can quickly fade if you discover that you are unable to restore the piece to a usable state. Make sure that you check the item thoroughly looking for problem areas. Don't forget to look inside and underneath as well.

There are some items out there that are completely unsalvageable, but most are redeemable depending upon the amount of time and effort you want to put into them. Listed here are some of the common injuries that you may find. You will have to decide whether or not they are worth overcoming.

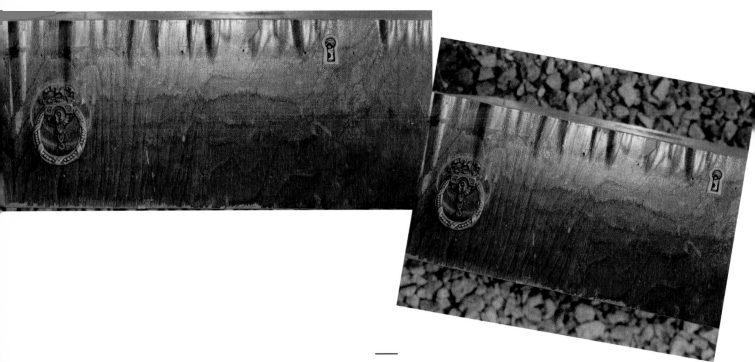

# Common Problems

❖ LEAD BASED PAINT This is probably the most prevalent problem you will encounter. It isn't difficult to refinish these pieces, but you do have to take precautions as lead paint is toxic. Anything produced around 1970 is likely to have lead based paint. Don't sand these items at all. Instead, use a liquid stripper. Always, use a mask. Finally, strip these items outside if at all possible where there is good ventilation and you don't have to worry about contaminating your work area.

❖ BLISTERED OR MISSING VENEER This can be a challenge, but not impossible to remedy. Glue can be injected into blistered veneer and pressed flat. If the original veneer comes off as a sheet, it can be glued back down as well. If the veneer is unusable, you can buy veneer at your local home center. It can be purchased in many different types of wood and can be cut to size and stained to match the rest of the piece. This can be tricky so you may have to practice on several pieces before you get it right.

❖ WOODWORM There are treatments for these critters though I have never felt the desire to bother with such pieces.

❖ LOOSE JOINTS Generally these can be easily fixed with wood glue and clamps.

❖ MISSING OR DAMAGED HARDWARE Obviously not a difficult problem to solve.

❖ DIRT Generally easy to fix, but be careful as water and detergents can dry out wood and raise the grain.

❖ RUST Removing rust from metal furniture takes a bit of elbow grease and it often requires getting into some awkward areas, but it can be done depending upon the extent. For surface rust removal, you will need wire brushes and steel wool. There are solvents such as naval jelly that remove rust that has penetrated deeply into metal, but they are very strong. Use these in areas with good ventilation and be certain to wear goggles and gloves to protect eyes and skin.

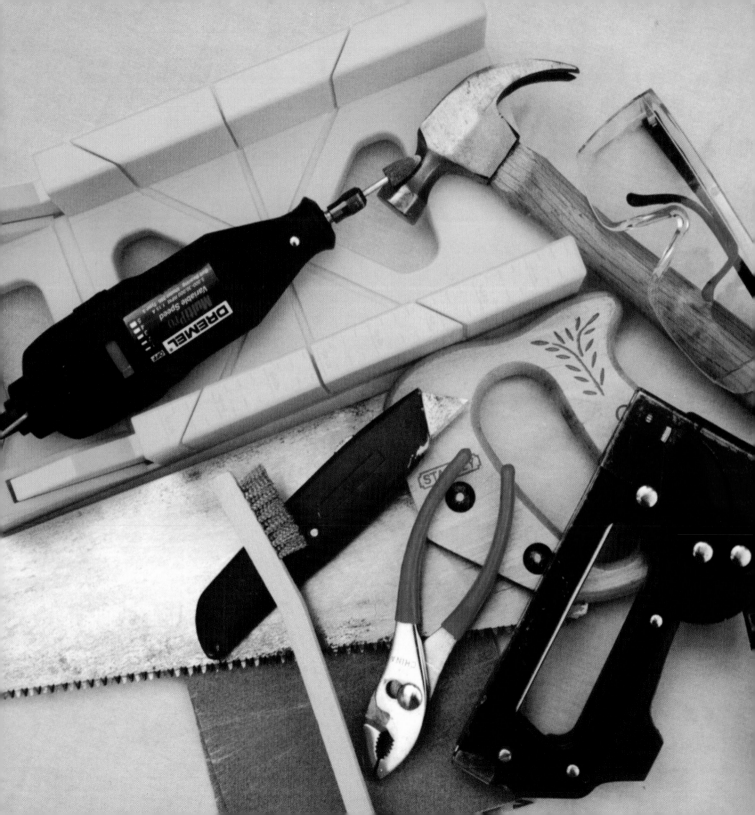

# The Tools

# Basic Tool Kit

Nothing slows down a project faster than having the wrong tools whereas having the proper tools will speed up and even improve the quality of the finished product. This section will provide you with the basic tool kit for most of the projects herein. However, there may be tools listed in the how-to section that may not be in your basic tool kit because it is a tool that you won't use on a regular basis. You may want to see if you can burrow or rent such tools. Furthermore, I'm a pretty thrifty person and it's likely that anyone refinishing flea market furniture is also a bargain hunter, but there's no bargain in cheaply made tools. When creating a basic tool box, don't buy the cheapest tools you can find. It's far better to pay a little more for a quality product than to get something that breaks the first time you use it. Always look at the guarantee offered by the manufacturer, as many will replace the item for free for the lifetime of the product. Finally, tools can be dangerous so please respect them. They are not for children so please keep them out of reach.

HAMMER Choose a simple claw hammer though many types are available. A wooden handled hammer is inexpensive and is good for most general repairs though metal and fiberglass are stronger. Choose one that is comfortable for you according to length and weight.

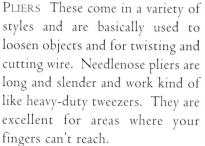

PLIERS These come in a variety of styles and are basically used to loosen objects and for twisting and cutting wire. Needlenose pliers are long and slender and work kind of like heavy-duty tweezers. They are excellent for areas where your fingers can't reach.

WRENCH This is a crescent or adjustable wrench, it is used to loosen or tighten nuts. Because it adjusts, it can accommodate various size nuts. Unlike pliers, a wrench will not slip as easily while you turn it.

SCREWDRIVERS The most common are flat head and Phillips. A flat head is straight and a Phillips has a cross on the tip. Find the right size for the screw; one that is too small may slip and strip the screw head while one that is too big may damage the area surrounding the screw.

TAPE MEASURE  A very recognizable tool, a 25ft. self-retracting tape measure is suitable for most do-it-yourselfers. Anything bigger is for the serious contractor.

HACK SAW  This saw is designed for making fine cuts. It can be used for metal or wood. It is important to make sure that the teeth of the blade face forward or your effort will be doubled.

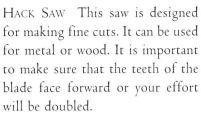
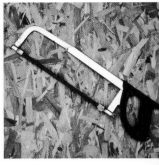

HAND SAW  A hand saw is just a good general tool to have around in the place of some of the specialized saws that can be used. It is only used to cut wood however and does not work well for finish or detail work.

MITER BOX  A miter box allows you cut precise angles and is a must if you ever plan to do anything with molding. They can be made of wood or steel. A compound miter saw is a power saw that can also perform similar functions.

STAPLE GUN  A staple gun, whether manual or electric, is great for projects such as reupholstering. New seat covers can be made in mere minutes with this tool.

PUTTY KNIFE  This very useful tool is used for patching holes in wood or in walls and is good for scraping purposes when stripping paint. Though they come in various widths, a good choice is one with a 1-inch blade and another with a 2 or 3-inch blade.

SCRAPER  This item holds a straight edge razor blade that retracts into the handle when not in use. It easily removes paint, stickers, and decals. Be careful, as the blades are incredibly sharp and can easily cut you or mar the surface of your furniture.

TAPE  With many types, it is best to choose the right tape for your job. Painter's tape comes up easily without pulling off paint. Masking tape is a good general tape. Duct tape is very strong and really stays put. Electrical tape is just that, for electrical projects.

WIRE BRUSH/STEEL WOOL These items are necessary when removing rust from metal. A wire brush is capable of getting into tight places and helps clean paint from your brushes. Steel wool is often the last abrasive used when sanding a surface.

PAINT PADS/BRUSHES These are rather obvious necessities, but recognize that the finishes each produce differ from one to another. Be sure that the material used to make the brush or pad is usable for the application. For example, don't use a foam pad with solvents.

SAND PAPER Sand paper is graded according to the coarseness. A low grade paper is very coarse and is used for rough sanding. It removes a lot of material quickly. Higher grades are less coarse and create a smoother surface. Higher grades are used for finish work.

WOOD GLUE Wood glue is important in the way it reacts with wood fibers. Some glues infiltrate wood fibers whereas some stay on the surface. Those that don't soak in take up space when they dry much like a putty. These may cause damage to surrounding areas.

UTILITY KNIFE A utility knife is just a good all around tool to have on hand. Whether you use it to open packaging, to cut twin, or to score wood, you will be glad to have this handy tool in your tool belt.

SAFETY GLASSES Many people hate wearing safety glasses for various reasons from discomfort to just plain looking silly, but safety glasses can save your vision. It's worth some discomfort or looking silly for such a precious commodity.

# Basic Power Tool Kit

There are precautions that should be taken with all tools. One is that you should always wear safety glasses when using these tools as you never know when something will fly back and hit you in the face. When using power tools, you should carefully examine the material to be used making sure that it is free of nails or other metal.

Finally, always pull the electric plug before you make any adjustments to the tool.

Power tools can be expensive so you may want to burrow these tools or rent them before you buy them. It is also important that you read all the instructions before use or have someone show you how to use it.

DRILL  Drills are useful for a variety of tasks. Old wood is dry and brittle. It may easily split if you don't predrill a hole to drive a screw. They are also great to power drive screws. You'll save a lot of time and energy if you learn to use this tool.

RANDOM ORBITAL SANDER  This type of sander is small and useful for furniture projects. Also a big time saver, it doesn't create directional marks on wood caused by the repetition of the sanding mechanism.

JIGSAW  A jigsaw isn't as intimidating as you might think and it is very useful to know how to operate one. It can be a good substitute for other more specialized saws as well. Just follow the manufacturer's instructions and be sure to take safety precautions including goggles.

ROTARY TOOL  This handy little tool can do a myriad of tasks depending upon the attachments used. You can purchase sanding disks, wire brush attachments, and mini saw blades. But it's for small areas only.

# Basic Refinishing Techniques

# Stripping Paint

The old adage that sometimes you have to destroy something to make it better is definitely the case here. One of the most common techniques used when refurbishing flea market or second-hand furniture is stripping paint. There are several reasons to do this. The current paint may be a garish color that no one can live with or the painted finish is chipped or otherwise marred. Sometimes, the piece may look better stained rather than painted. Another problem could be that the piece has been painted so many times, that it just needs to be stripped in order to get the cleanest finish. In any case, it isn't typically difficult as far as skill is concerned, but it can be very tedious and time consuming.

There are a myriad of stripping products on the market. They come in aerosols, liquids, gels, and non-aerosol sprays. It's best to consult your hardware store to find out which is best for your application until you've gained some experience.

Once you've chosen a stripper, be sure that you have protective gloves, steel wool, paint brushes, and a small putty knife to scrape off the old finish. A small stiff brush or old toothbrush works well for detailed areas and hard-to-reach crevices. A good way to do turned legs is to use a shoe string or strip of coarse cloth to wrap around and then pull back and forth as if buffing shoes. There is no need for a mask as it will not protect you from fumes. Therefore, it is important to use stripping solutions in a well-ventilated area—outside whenever possible. Use the stripper in a hidden area of the item to make sure it doesn't harm the material. Finally, always read and follow the manufacturer's instructions for proper use and check your area codes for disposal of the product and the stripped paint.

Read the manufacturer's instructions for your specific stripper. Gloves protect your hands, but most masks don't protect you from fumes. Use in a well ventilated area. Try the product in a concealed area of your furniture before doing the entire piece to see how it reacts.

Using an old toothbrush, remove paint from hard-to-reach or detailed areas. Use caution as the brush may flick stripper which is especially dangerous if it gets on your skin or in your eyes. Shoe strings work well for turned legs. Just wrap around and pull on each end as if buffing.

Some strippers come with a spray bottle. Others can be poured into a glass jar and dabbed on with a brush. Working on a small section at a time, apply a thick layer of stripper onto the painted surface. Allow for it to activate according to the manufacturer's instructions.

When the recommended time has passed, the paint will bubble and the layers can be stripped away using a putty knife. Always push the knife away from yourself. Wipe your tools on a rag or into a container that can be easily disposed of afterward.

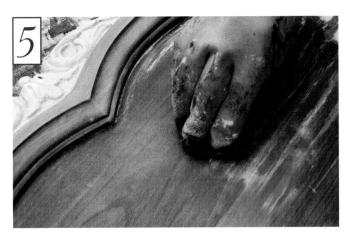

Remove any remaining residue using steel wool soaked in stripper. Rub until the item is clear of paint, turning or replacing the steel wool once it becomes full of paint. Afterward, use a clean piece of steel wool and wipe with denatured alcohol to remove the stripper residue.

Once the stripper has dried, use a fine-grit sand paper to sand the surface. This creates a smooth surface and removes any paint that may still remain on the item. Use a tack cloth to remove the dust before refinishing.

# Repainting

By the time you finish stripping a piece of junk furniture, you may be ready to collapse in a heap, but the truth is that you're only half way home. After you've stripped the old finish away, you must apply a new one.

Basic repainting is not a difficult task, but to make the most of your hard work, go the extra distance and do it well. First, you must choose a color. Get paint chips from the hardware store, and bring them home to view in the same light in which you will view your furniture item. Note that the white border around most paint chips causes colors to appear more vibrant. To help alleviate this, cut off the white border and only look at the color that you are considering.

Next, consider whether you need latex or oil-based paint. Latex paint is generally the easiest to use. It dries quickly and cleans up with water. With the proper preparations, it also holds up under use. Oil-based paints are noxious and are harsh on you and the environment. They also require chemicals for clean up. Oil-based paints are better for items such as metal furniture, floors or for some outdoor applications, but generally latex is just as durable and much more user-friendly.

Once you've chosen a paint, don't forget the primer. Primer protects the wood and creates a stable surface on which to paint so that the furniture is less likely to chip or have color variations. It may seem that primer is just an added expense, but you can actually save on the amount of paint used if you prime first especially on bare wood surfaces because they won't soak up as much paint. Latex primer is good for furniture that you don't plan to strip, but on which you want to provide a stable surface. For furniture that you've stripped or that you bought unfinished, oil-based primer is best as latex has water in it that can raise the grain of unfinished wood.

Finally, before applying the primer, remove dust with a dry cloth or tack cloth. Don't use anything damp as it will raise the grain of the wood. Once the primer is dry, sand with a fine-grit sandpaper and wipe again with a tack cloth. Stir your paint to mix. Paint the furniture item with enough coats that you have a nice even color and smooth finish.

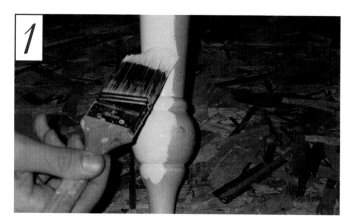

Before priming, make sure the surface is dust free by wiping with a dry cloth or tack cloth. Then prime the surface using a thick-bristled paint brush.

When the primer is dry, sand the item lightly with fine-grit sandpaper following the grain of the wood. Again, wipe with a tack cloth. Stir your paint to mix and then paint in the direction of the wood.

# Staining

Another finishing option is staining. Stains come in a myriad of colors with the most common being shades of brown. However, they do come in a variety of vibrant colors such as red, green and blue. Check out your local hardware store to see what they carry.

After stripping a piece of furniture, be sure to sand with a fine-grit sand paper. Then wipe the surface with a dry cloth or a tack cloth to remove dust. Depending upon the piece and the look you desire, use a wood bleach (found at your hardware store) to even out any color variations. The bleach removes any previous color left behind from the old stain or paint. Follow the manufacturer's instructions if you choose to use a wood bleach. Because the ingredients are very caustic, be certain to use protective gear including long rubber gloves and safety goggles. Long sleeves and pants are good, too. After applying the wood bleach, wipe down the entire surface with a mild vinegar and water solution to remove any residue.

You can apply stain using a paint brush, paint pad, clean rag or staining pad. Stir the stain before applying. Apply it in the the direction of the grain. Allow it to dry according to the manufacturer's instructions. Apply successive coats depending upon the amount of color you desire.

Follow up any staining project with a coat of polyurethane, oil-based varnish or furniture wax to provide a protective finish. Polyurethane and varnish are best applied with paint pads in thin layers to avoid bubbles. Lightly sand with a fine steel wool pad and tack cloth between each layer. Wax can be applied with a soft cloth or steel wool depending upon whether you desire a weathered appearance or a more refined finish.

Before staining, wipe the surface with a tack cloth to remove dirt. Then apply the stain using a brush, pad or cloth in the direction of the grain. Apply in layers until the desired color is attained.

Follow up by coating with a sealer such as polyurethane, varnish or furniture wax to protect the finish and the wood. Apply polyurethane in at least two thin coats. Lightly sand and wipe with tack cloth between coats.

# Bagged Finish

A bagged finish is a faux finish technique that uses a scrunched up plastic bag to apply paint to a surface. It gives the surface a soft muted texture with varying tones. This finish generally looks best on large flat surfaces such as a headboard of a bed. It can also be used on a wall.

As with many finishes, a bagged finish makes use of a base and top coat of paint. Of course, this basic technique can be made more complicated with a number of layers, but here we utilize only the base layer and top layer. These layers can be any two colors. As the colors are intermingled, it is best to try your color combination on a spare piece of cardstock or wood to make sure that the colors work well together. Otherwise, you may find that they clash or become a muddy mess. Generally, it is best to use colors that are related on the color wheel (see page 39) or a few shades of the same color. In our example, we use a light green base coat and darker green top coat. This creates a soothing finish.

When bagging, be sure to turn the grocery bag inside out so that the writing doesn't come off on your project. Have plenty of bags on hand as they may need to be changed out for new ones after awhile depending upon the size of your project. A smaller project may require that you cut up the bag and use smaller sections, so again, try your technique on a scrap piece of wood or paper before starting.

Finally, you can experiment with glazes to further soften the appearance of the paint. Glazes can be pretinted or can be tinted using various mixtures of glaze and paint. The more glaze in the mixture, the more transparent the paint will be. Note that glaze increases the time it takes for the paint to dry.

First, paint the item with a base color using a paint brush. After applying a base color, turn a plastic shopping bag inside out so that the ink is on the inside. Scrunch up the bag and dip it into the second color. Blot the excess paint off onto a rag to avoid using too much paint.

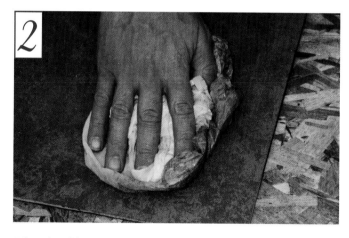

Then briskly pounce the bag over the surface, varying the angle so as not to have a defined pattern.

# Sponge Finish

A sponged finish is a faux finish technique that uses a sea sponge to apply paint to a surface. It is very similar to the bagged finish technique. Like a bagged finish, it gives the surface a muted texture with varying tones. It also looks best on large flat surfaces such as a headboard of a bed, and this technique can be used on a wall just like the bagged finish technique.

A sponged finish also utilizes a base and top coat of paint, though you can use any number of colors and layers depending upon your skill and goal. Again, try your color combination on a spare piece of cardstock or wood to make sure that the colors work well together. See the color wheel (on page 39) for color ideas.

A sea sponge is best for sponging as other types of manufactured sponges have a distinct texture that is obvious in the finished project. A sea sponge is much more random and doesn't create a pattern as readily as a manufactured sponge. When sponging, be sure to blot the sponge on an old rag each time before using it to apply the paint. Otherwise, it has a tendency to pick up a lot of paint and distribute a large blob of paint on your project the first time you touch it to the surface. Also, this technique is somewhat messy. Wear old clothes and rubber gloves. After awhile and depending on the size of your project, you may need to rinse out your sponge. A smaller project may require that you cut or tear up a large sponge.

Once again, you can experiment with glazes to make the paint less opaque.

After applying a base color, dip a natural sponge in a second color. Blot off the excess paint.

Briskly bounce the sponge over the surface, varying the angle so as not to have a defined pattern. You may repeat this step using a third or even fourth complimentary color usually in the same color palette.

# Crackle Finish

A crackle finish is just one of the many ways to create a sense of age about an item, but also just for fun. Over time, paint breaks down. It crazes and peels revealing the previous layers of paint before it. Sometimes the paint breaks down to the point of seeing bare wood. This is the effect that crackle compound tries to emulate. Manufacturers have created many types of crazing and crackling compounds depending on the effect desired. Some create a finish more like aging paint on wood whereas other compounds create an effect similar to the way porcelain glaze crazes over time. Which one you choose is up to you and the materials you wish to imitate.

As with all the techniques shown in this book, it is best to practice on a scrap of wood or in a hidden place on the furniture to determine which color combinations to use and how it will look. Crackle compounds require a base finish and top finish. Generally, both the base and top coats are painted, but you can begin with a base coat that is stained. The colors for the base and top coats can be as varied as the paint colors available. You don't have to stay historically accurate when using this technique so it can be anything your heart desires.

Finally, crackle compounds require that you apply the compound and then wait for a certain length of time to let it cure. This prescribed amount of time varies by manufacturer and the effect desired. The minimum amount of time, generally results in a wider crackling effect revealing a great deal of the base coat. The maximum amount of time results in a finer less noticeable crazing effect that shows less of the base coat.

After priming, apply the base coat.

Apply the crackling compound and follow the manufacturer's instructions on how long to let stand.

Apply the second color. Do not "play" with the paint much. Simply lay the paint on and let it go. Don't try to make it perfect or you will smear it.

# Antiqued Finish

An antiqued finish is somewhat vague as it really is a combination of various other finishes to create an overall suggestion of age. Antiquing a piece of furniture can involve various finishes in any number of combinations. Some general rules do apply.

First, when using paint, start with a color that might have been used decades ago. No matter how you try, you can't make hot pink look old. Many paint manufacturers have come out with lines of paint that are closely related to those that historians have researched and have found to be historically accurate.

Second, you want to replicate signs of wear in areas that would actually have gotten worn. Sanding away paint in areas for no apparent reason will tip people off that the piece really isn't old, and furthermore, was refinished. Think about how you use a piece of furniture: how do you touch it; what comes in contact with it; what areas are most prone to be touched. Areas that protrude often become worn because they are most likely to get rubbed and banged by passersby, etc. Certain edges such as the front edge or corners are likely to become worn as they are more vulnerable than back edges and corners that may be placed near a wall. Areas around handles, knobs, and pulls are likely to become worn as people open and close doors and drawers thus wearing away paint.

Finally, no matter how well we clean, grime builds up in cracks and crevices. And areas subjected to cleaning products as well as sun and light will likely lighten in color over time. When applying an antiquing glaze, be sure that you wipe away most of it on flat surfaces and on the areas that protrude, but leave some behind in cracks and crevices or in the low points of carvings and other detail work. Use wax to protect the finish.

Rubbing candle wax on areas that are typically worn will cause an area to resist paint. Paint with traditional colors. Use steel wool to subtly sand areas where furniture naturally ages such as near handles and edges. Use antiquing glaze or stain to discolor newly exposed wood.

Apply a small amount of antiquing glaze. Wipe off excess on flat areas and on high points, but leave behind more glaze in the cracks and crevices. The amount of glaze you leave behind is up to you. You can use steel wool to buff away some finish on the high points if desired.

# Distressed Finish

A distressed finish is generally associated with an antiqued piece as it typically gives an air of age. Why else would you have worn areas, nail holes, and dents-- unless you have kids that is. As a rule, distressed finishes are great for families with small children. No one will notice the toy truck than was driven into the front corner or the slight pigmentation left behind after cleaning up crayon scribbles. Distressed finishes are low-key friendly finishes that age gracefully. Like antique finishes, a distressed finish can be created with various combinations of other techniques, but unlike antiquing, you generally don't have to worry as much with the style or colors because you aren't necessarily looking to be historically accurate or to "fool" the eye. You just want to give the impression that the item is a well-loved piece of furniture.

As a rule, areas that stick out or have a higher relief are the areas that get banged up and worn down. These are the areas on which you also want to concentrate your efforts. You never know how something may have gotten roughed up moving from one house to another, how kids may have reeked havoc, how pets may have scratched the surface. An unexpected flaw here or there can add interest, but don't overdo it. Otherwise, it will still seem like a piece of junk after all your hard work.

Finally, don't feel as if you need to follow a prescribed set of rules and don't try to get everything perfect. Again, you aren't trying to give the impression that the piece is antique, just well-loved.

Distressing often incorporates a variety of finishes such as crackled and antiqued. It's a creative process -- choose which combination of elements to use and when to stop. If working on a new piece of unfinished furniture, a good place to start is by staining or painting it.

Paint the object again in a contrasting color. Then buff the paint off on edges and other protrusions that would normally see wear over years of use. The candle wax will make this task easier. If you chose to use crackle compound, you will see the base color through the second layer of paint.

Rub candle wax where you characteristically see wear and tear such as near handles, on relief work, and on edges. The wax keeps subsequent layers of paint from adhering to the surface. Rub paint off of these ares with fine steel wool for a worn appearance.

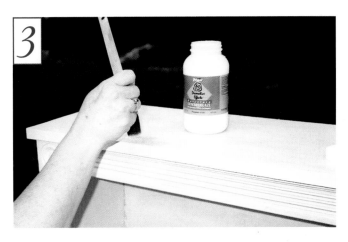

Another option is to apply a crackle finish over the first color of paint. The crackle finish makes the paint appear older than it is revealing the base color through the crackle.

A quintessential step to this look is to produce the illusion of age and wear by using a bag of bolts, hammer, etc. to "beat up" or "distress" the surface. This mimics years of moving catastrophes, bumps from toy trucks, and general wear and tear. This furniture is very kid-friendly.

Apply an antiquing glaze in the cracks and crevices to give the appearance of buildup from dirt, wax, etc. Leave behind some glaze in corners, molding, nicks and dents. Use furniture wax to create a protective finish. Wax resists paint, so make this your last step.

# Stenciling

Stenciling is as easy or as difficult as you make it. Stencils are made of a variety of materials including plastic and metal and some can have multiple layers in order to accomplish an overall design The more layers, the more difficult. Paints range from liquid to pastes.

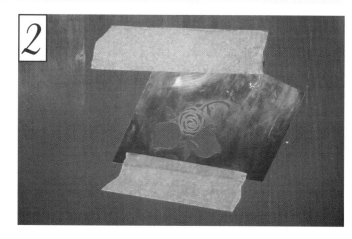

Use painters tape to help secure the stencil in place. Painters tape is more easily removed than other types and it won't peel away any finishes underneath it as some other types of tapes may do.

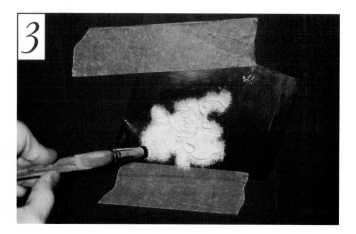

Load a stencil brush with paint and then pounce onto a scrap piece of fabric to get rid of any excess paint. Gently pounce the brush onto the stencil cutout being careful not to let the paint bleed under the stencil.

Fill in the area or highlight the shape by only doing the edges. Repeat this process with different colors if desired, but clean the stencil and brush between colors. Peel away the stencil when complete.

# Color Wheel

The color wheel shown below is a great tool for determining color combinations. Color is such an important consideration and can completely change the feel of a project or room. Pay particular attention to the use of color when beginning any project.

Primary colors are red, yellow and blue. All other colors are a mixture of these three colors. Secondary colors are orange, green and purple.

Some colors are considered warm. These are shades of reds, oranges and yellows. Other colors have a cool appearance and are shades of blue, greens, and purples.

Colors on opposite sides of the wheel are called complimentary colors. An important characteristic of these colors is that they tend to exaggerate the intensity of one another thereby causing them to appear brighter than if they were alone or with other colors. For example, red and green are on opposite sides of the wheel. They are complimentary colors and appear very bright when used together. Think of Christmas decorations and how brilliant the reds and greens appear when they are used in the same vicinity. The same red will look completely different when used with blue or orange for example.

Another important aspect of complimentary colors is that they create brown when mixed. Be careful when using them in the same project making sure paint dries between steps.

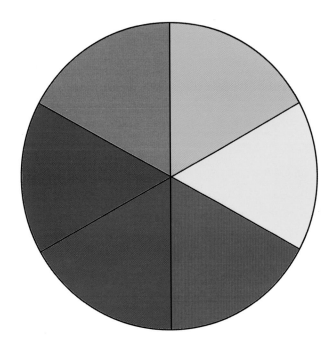

# How to Use a Miter Box

A miter cut is a cut made on an angle so that two pieces can come together to form a corner. Think of a picture frame. The corners of the frame are mitered at 45° angles so that when they are put together, they create a square. Two tools are used to make miter cuts—a miter box or a power miter saw. A miter box is simply a frame or template that has precut guides for your hand saw. You place the wood in the frame and use the corresponding guide to cut it at the angle you need.

The advantage of a miter box is that it is low tech and inexpensive. A power miter saw is very intimidating for the beginner and can be expensive depending upon the features and size, but it makes more accurate cuts and is capable of repeating the same cut quickly and uniformly.

It is wise to practice a cut on a scrap piece of wood before cutting your molding so that you don't make costly mistakes. Figuring out which way the angle needs to go is the hardest part. Otherwise, adding molding is a quick and easy way of dressing up lots of things from window and door frames to walls and furniture, so it is helpful to know how to use a miter box.

First determine the angle that you need to cut. A 90° cut is a straight cut. A 45° cut is when one piece of molding runs directly into another creating a square corner. The 45° and the 90° cuts are the most common cuts you will make.

Second, determine the type of corner—inside or outside. The kind of corner needed plays an important role in mitering. An outside corner is when the corner protrudes (shown here in pink). An inside corner is when the corner recedes into a space (shown here in blue).

Remember that there are several things that can alter the results of the cut.

1) Whether the molding is laying face up or face down.

2) Whether the molding is laying on its edge or on its face.

3) The slot in which you put your saw.

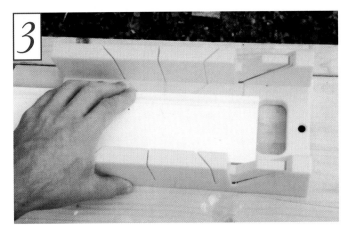

To cut a 45º angle, lay the molding in the miter box. Press it against the bottom and outside wall of the miter box.

Slide your hand saw into the angled guide. Holding the wood firmly, cut the wood with the emphasis on the push stroke letting the slot guide your saw.

# Inspiring Ideas for Flea Market Finds

# Coffee Table

This outdated table was once a small dinette table and is commonly found in inexpensive department stores. The top was scratched and the color was quite yellowed, not to mention that it was tiny as far as dining was concerned. However, it was solid wood and had a charming design. The fold down leaves were still in good working order. Overall, it was a good purchase. Because this wasn't really a table that anyone wanted for dining purposes any longer, I chose to make it into a coffee table that I could use in my family room.

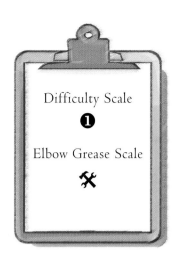

Difficulty Scale

❶

Elbow Grease Scale

⚒

MATERIALS
primer
paint color of choice
antiquing glaze
polyurethane

TOOLS
wrench
screwdriver
tape measure
painter's/masking tape
wood saw
paint brushes/pads
orbital sander
sand paper
tack cloth

First, remove the legs using a wrench. Measure each leg and mark it according to the desired length. Measure and mark in several places. A grease pencil marks easily and comes off easily as well.

If you don't have a compound miter saw, place a piece of tape around the leg and cut off with a hand saw, trying to stay in line with the tape or else you may end up with uneven bottoms. Sand afterward until even.

Next, remove any other hardware that may remain on the table top including the leaves. It is up to you whether to remove the supports for the leaf mechanism depending upon its type.

Once the hardware is removed, strip the existing finish if you plan to stain it. Otherwise, scuff the surface with sand paper so that the paint will stick. Wipe with a damp cloth or tack cloth. Prime if necessary.

Apply your desired finish. This table was painted. Use a stiff bristled brush, the cheapest you can find, to create the streaks. You may choose another type of finish.

After the paint dried thoroughly, this table was antiqued using antiquing glaze. Then replace the hardware and legs. Then apply wax or polyurethane for a durable finish.

# Mosaic Side Table

This small table was of little use without its top. The top wasn't a solid piece and it had a picture frame effect. Such a table isn't needed for this project though as any table would do with the addition of some simple molding. With this table, the broken china fit right into the recessed top.

Difficulty Scale

❶ ❷

Elbow Grease Scale

✗ ✗

**Materials**
plywood
1 ½in finishing nails
thin set tile adhesive
grout
tiles or pieces of broken
  china
grout sealer

**Tools**
tape measure
jigsaw
sand paper
tile trowel
grout float
sponge
bucket

Wash the piece removing loose paint with a scrub brush. If this is for a child's room, remove any lead paint on the table.

Turn the table over and measure the inside of the opening to determine the size of the top.

Cut out an insert according to the measurements from the underside of the opening. This can be done from laminated plywood or solid wood. Fit the piece to make sure it is the correct size. Make adjustments if necessary.

Secure the new top on the underside of the opening using a brace. Glue it and nail it into place. Finish as desired.

Apply thin set tile cement to the table top using a tile trowel. Use the notches on the trowel to spread the cement. Apply whole or broken tiles or china into the cement randomly or in a pattern. Be sure the pieces are roughly level with no edges sticking up. Allow the thin set to dry according to the manufacturer's instructions.

Once the thin set is dry, apply grout between the pieces. According to the manufacturer's instructions, wipe off excess grout with a damp sponge (against the grain) rinsing the sponge between wipes. Do this until the tiles have no haze when dry. Once the grout is dry as per the manufacturer's instructions, seal with grout sealer to prevent stains.

# Kitchen Island

Kitchen islands are a staple in today's kitchens and for good reason. They are the perfect place to store kitchen appliances, to prepare food, or to just sit and have some toast in the morning. They can be as complex or as simple as desired. They can match or compliment the cabinets. They can be fixed into position or they can be made portable. They are also simple to make out of kitchen cabinets or other old pieces of furniture. Here we convert an old desk.

**Materials**
primer
stripper
paint color of choice
1 pine laminate board
wood screws
4 legs
4 wheels (optional)
mineral oil

**Tools**
putty knife
wood saw
jigsaw
tape measure
screwdriver
drill and bits
tack cloth
paint brushes/pads

Clean the desk removing loose paint.

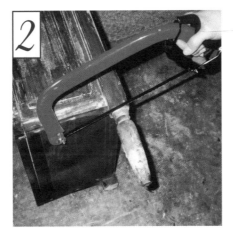

Remove the existing legs as these will be replaced with new ones later. Remove the top of the desk as well and put aside.

Measure the bottom of the desk. Using these measurements, cut one piece of pine laminate the same size and attach to the bottom of the desk with screws in all four corners.

The island needs to be about 36 inches tall when complete. Determine the length of the legs by subtracting the height thus far from 36. Keep in mind the height of wheels if you choose. Predrill a hole in each leg if needed and screw the leg into the island. Predrill holes in the bottom of the legs and insert the rollers if you choose.

Refinish the desk and legs in a uniform color. Do not paint the top.

Strip the old top. Use 1 part bleach to 2 parts water to even out the color. Then sand again. Rub with mineral oil to finish. Secure it to the island with adhesive and screws from the underside. Other materials such as solid surfacing, butcherblock, natural stone or laminate countertop can also be used for the top depending on its purpose.

# Bathroom Vanity

Like many people, my husband and I wanted our new house to have the character and warmth of an old farmhouse. When searching for a vanity for our master bath, we decided to look for an old chest of drawers to convert into the vanity. There are scores of dressers out there. You just need to consider if you want one sink or two and make sure it fits your space. Other types of furniture that work well for this purpose are dry sinks and buffets. Buffets are especially good if you want two sinks as they are typically longer than chest of drawers. Another option for this project would be to have a solid surface top or natural stone top made to fit your dresser. Then you would simply replace the top of the dresser with the new top and drop in the sink basin.

Difficulty Scale

❶❷❸❹❺

Elbow Grease Scale

✖✖✖✖✖

**Materials**
stripper
primer if painting
paint or stain color of
    choice
polyurethane
basin
faucet
plumbing materials
wood glue
caulk

**Tools**
sand paper
drill and bits
jigsaw
tack cloth
paint brushes/pads

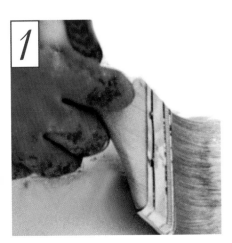

First, strip the existing finish if desired. You may want to use wood bleach to even out the tones. If you are painting it, then there is no need.

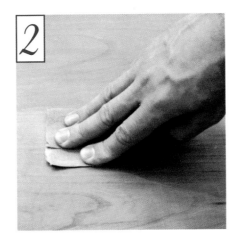

Use fine-grit sandpaper to smooth the surface. This is a big project so a power sander comes in handy for the large areas. Wipe with a slightly damp cloth or tack cloth to remove dust.

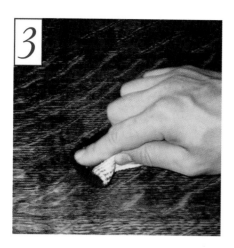

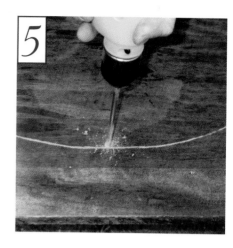

Paint or stain as desired. Once dry, apply three layers of polyurethane scuffing the finish between each application. Polyurethane is critical as it protects the wood from water damage in this wet environment.

Choose a basin that will fit the width and depth of your dresser. Also consider the space needed for the faucet. Use the template given with the sink basin to mark the opening of the sink.

Drill a starter hole for the jig saw blade. Place the hole just inside the template line.

After removing the drawers, use a jig saw to cut the opening. Begin where the starter hole was drilled. Duct tape placed on the guide of the saw will prevent scratching the surface as the saw cuts along the line.

Once the opening is cut, be sure to polyurethane the opening to protect it from water damage as well. Drill holes for the faucet. Drop in the sink and plumb as you would a purchased vanity.

You probably need to rework the drawers if the plumbing gets in the way. Disassemble, cut the drawer to length and reassemble. You may have to give up the top drawers completely, but the bottom ones can usually be salvaged.

# Dresser

I first bought this dresser to turn into a bathroom vanity, but decided against it later in favor of a less ornate dresser. That left me with this dresser that I then chose to use in my daughter's bedroom. The veneer was missing on the small center and bottom drawers. The veneer from the small center drawer was in good condition and was reapplied using spray adhesive. The veneer on the bottom drawer was replaced with new veneer purchased through a mail order company which was then stained to match.

Difficulty Scale
❶ ❷

Elbow Grease Scale

⚒ ⚒

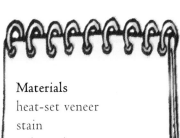

**Materials**
heat-set veneer
stain
polyurethane
wood putty

**Tools**
putty knife
orbital sander
sand paper
utility knife
household iron
roller
tack cloth
paint brushes/pads

Remove any remaining veneer. It may simply peel off or you may need to use a putty knife or chisel. What doesn't come off, sand off. This is tedious, but you must remove all traces of the old veneer.

Once the old veneer is gone, sand the drawer front to make a good even surface for the new veneer. Wipe with a tack cloth.

Fill any dents, holes, etc. with wood putty. Push the putty into the hole with a putty knife. Allow to dry. Then sand flush with the face of the drawer.

Cut pieces of the new veneer so that it overhangs the edges on all sides by 1 inch. The grain of the new veneer should run in the same direction as that on the remainder of the dresser. Using a household iron on low (check the manufacturer's instructions) apply the veneer by ironing it never stopping in one area which may cause scorching.

After heating the entire piece, roll over every section firmly to be sure it makes contact. Begin in the center and roll toward the edge. A smooth flat block of wood that you rub over the surface works as well.

Once the veneer cools, trim the excess veneer using a utility knife and a new blade. Then carefully drill the holes for the handles according to what had previously been there. Stain the veneer to match. Then polyurethane or wax depending upon the finish of the remainder of the dresser.

# Victorian Dressing Table

Difficulty Scale

❶❷

Elbow Grease Scale

⚒ ⚒

This dressing table was actually "rescued" from my grandmother's attic. Yes, I know that isn't a flea market find exactly, but the techniques used to liven up this vanity can be used with many flea market or yard sale finds. My great-grandmother purchased this dressing table as part of a suite when she was a young woman. As it had quite a lovely patina, I chose to keep most of the original finish and just restore some trouble areas. The worst areas were the horizontal surfaces on which people placed various items over the years as well as a broken leg.

**Materials**
stripper
stain
furniture wax
wood glue

**Tools**
paint brushes/pads
putty knife
painter's tape
sand paper/steel wool
tack cloth
cotton swabs
polishing rag

Start by cleaning with a mild furniture or oil soap being careful not to use too much water or it could actually do further damage.

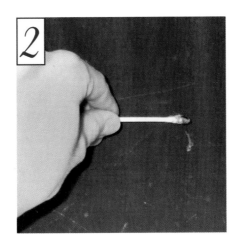

Touch up scratches with a cotton swab and matching stain.

This vanity had a broken leg. Make sure breaks are free of dirt. Use wood glue on both sides. Using painter's tape, secure the broken piece in place until dried.

The flat surfaces were the only areas to be striped entirely. Apply the stripper being careful to only apply it where it is wanted.

Start and stop at "natural" points to help trick the eye in the final finish. Such starting/stopping points may be edges, or where stain/paint colors change, etc. as shown here in blue.

After stripping the area, clean it of stripping agents by wiping with denatured alcohol. Paint or stain it to blend the new finish with the original. Afterward, polyurethane or wax to protect and revive the luster.

# $\mathcal{L}$inen Closet

This linen closet was once a bachelor's wardrobe. There are two sides to this wardrobe. On the left were shelves where he once put his folded clothes and on the right was a rod were he could hang his clothes facing out. I don't know if that was it's original purpose, but this older gentleman explained how it was one of the few pieces of furniture that he owned as a young man and he kept it all those years. There were extra nails in it so that he could hang cloths on the nail heads and the molding on the top had even been cut so that it could fit snugly again a wall. It used to be very plain and hum drum, but I saw it as the perfect linen closet for a tight space in my master bath.

Difficulty Scale
❶❷❸

Elbow Grease Scale
✗✗✗

**Materials**
primer
paint (2 colors of
    choice)
crackle compound
shelving boards
adjustable shelving
shelf pins

**Tools**
pliers
orbital sander
sand paper
tape measure
jigsaw
drill and bits
tack cloth
paint brushes/pads

Clean such items inside and out. Then pull out any extra nails, staples, etc. and remove the hardware. Scuff the surface with sand paper if painting or strip if staining. Then wipe with a tack cloth. Begin with primer.

Then apply a base color. This piece was painted periwinkle as the base color. Choose any combination appropriate to your decor.

Following the manufacturer's instructions, apply the crackle compound on top of the base color and wait the appropriate amount of time for it to cure.

After waiting the prescribed amount of time, apply the top coat of paint. The top coat of this wardrobe was an ink blue. The top coat will crackle showing the base color.

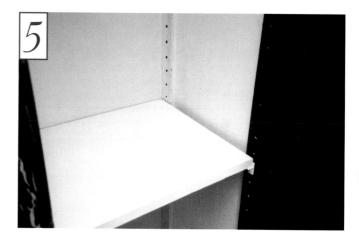

This item already had holes for shelving. Otherwise, you can purchase shelving brackets. Another option is to make brackets with strips of wood and a drill creating equally spaced holes and then applying the strips inside. Measure the inside dimensions for the shelves and cut to size.

# $\mathcal{P}$antry

I rescued this old cupboard from a basement. Because the house was heated with a coal furnace, the tall cupboard was covered in 25 years of coal dust and was filled with canning jars and equipment and old storage items. It's shelves were covered in printed contact paper. It was difficult to see what a beautiful piece of furniture it was, but the owner knew the person who handmade it from planking and explained how it had gotten the large chip in the top corner molding. My husband thought I was crazy when I told him I wanted to make it into a pantry for our kitchen, but he was pleasantly surprised with the results and we've gotten many compliments on it.

Difficulty Scale

❶

Elbow Grease Scale

⚒ ⚒

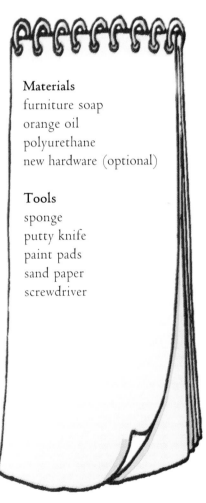

**Materials**
furniture soap
orange oil
polyurethane
new hardware (optional)

**Tools**
sponge
putty knife
paint pads
sand paper
screwdriver

Use a heavy duty detergent and scrub brush to wash it inside and out. Wipe it down with a large, heavy duty sponge as you go so the water doesn't seep into the wood. Change the water frequently so it doesn't redeposit the grime.

Kitchen items often have some sort of shelf liners or contact paper on them. Peel it away in pieces. The slower and more deliberate you are, the larger the pieces will be. The contact paper may leave a residue behind from the glue. If this is the case, you can wash the shelves with a detergent or with a product that contains orange oil.

After the cupboard is clean and free from contact paper, choose your finish. This cupboard had too much character to paint and the various types of wood were already beautiful shades of warm brown.

To protect the cupboard, use oil-based varnish or polyurethane. Its surface is too rough for wax. Flat, low gloss polyurethane was used to retain the primitive character. Remember to use thin layers to avoid getting bubbles.

Once the finish is completed, repair any missing or damaged hardware. The hinges on this cupboard needed adjustments so that the doors would close properly. The original latch was returned to its door.

# Chifforobe

This chifforobe was my grandparents'. It had seen better days. I remember playing in my grandparents' guest bedroom and how we used to open the mirrored door by jamming something in between the door and the frame, as the door had no knob and the skeleton key was missing. That caused significant damage to the wood frame. Nevertheless, I saw it as a link to my past and chose to bring it down out of it's seclusion and turn it into an entertainment and clothing armoire in my own bedroom. Any chifforobe or wardrobe can be similarly outfitted with ease.

Difficulty Scale
❶❷❸

Elbow Grease Scale
✖✖✖

**Materials**
stain
paint grade plywood
veneer edging
shelf pins
wood glue

**Tools**
screwdriver
tape measure
orbital sander
sand paper
tack cloth
household iron
drill and bits
clamps if necessary

First, clean it and remove the doors and hardware.

Next, measure the inside dimensions of the hanging side of the chifforobe. Measure all four sides as the item may no longer be square. Cut shelves to fit.

Use the manufactured edge as the front as it will be the cleanest cut. Cut the veneer 2 inches longer that the length of the shelf so that it overhangs on each end. Use a household iron to apply the veneer edging. The iron should be set on low so it melts the adhesive on the back but doesn't scorch the wood. Stain to match.

To use a shelf for a TV or stereo, measure the height of the object and add 2 inches for air circulation. Otherwise, just measure the desired height between shelves and drill the holes for shelf pins accordingly.

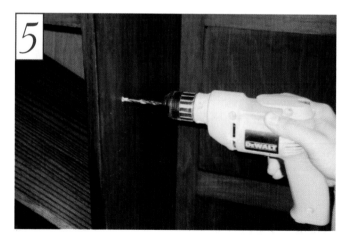

If the sides of the chifforobe are solid, drill holes for shelf pins. You can make as many holes as you need, but be sure to measure out the placement for each to be certain that the shelf isn't crooked once installed. Tape on the drill bit shows when the hole is deep enough.

Repair any problem drawers with wood glue and clamps.

# Oak Rocking Chair

This antique rocker had seen better days, but the details were quite beautiful for such a good price. I knew it would be great to sit by the fire. What better way to soothe one's soul than to quitely rock away stresses by the fire? A similar rocker might be just as well suited for a child's nursery or den.

Difficulty Scale

❶

Elbow Grease Scale

⚒

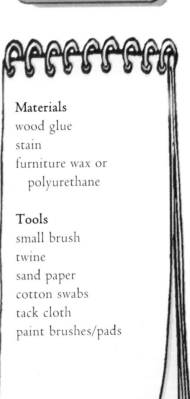

**Materials**
wood glue
stain
furniture wax or
    polyurethane

**Tools**
small brush
twine
sand paper
cotton swabs
tack cloth
paint brushes/pads

Clean all the joints of dirt and debris. Use a small brush to get into crevices and the holes.

Use wood glue to secure the spindles in place. Use a rag to wipe away any glue that oozes out of the joint when pressed together.

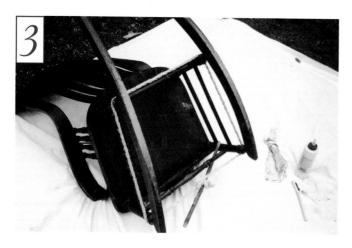

Bind the chair using twine to keep everything pulled together until the glue dries. To make the rope tight, tie a knot in the ends of the rope and insert a stick into the knot. Then twist the rope onto itself until tight. Tuck the stick under a spindle or into a crevice to hold it until dry.

Touch up any scratches or gouges with fine-grit sand paper and matching stain. Always sand in the same direction as the grain.

The seat of this rocker needed extra attention. It was very worn with splinters. Sand such areas until smooth to avoid injury. Then stain to match.

Seal with a coat of furniture wax. Wax the entire piece to help revive the wood.

# Child's Rocking Chair

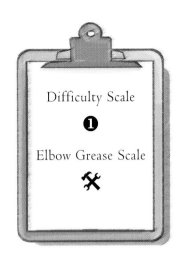

This rocking chair was mine growing up, but I have seen countless comparable chairs at yard sales, garage sales, flea markets and even new ones in craft chains. It is a simple rocking chair and thus, quite timeless. That's exactly why I like it. This one was missing a slat in the seat at one point, but it was repaired long ago. It wasn't perfect, but it had the potential to be a great little chair for my daughter's bedroom as well as a good place to read a book.

**Materials**
primer
paint
small bottles of
    acrylic paint in
    various colors
polyurethane

**Tools**
scrub brush
artist paint brushes
sand paper

*1*

Prepare the surface by cleaning the chair with a mild detergent. Make sure you get into all the tiny crevices. Use a toothbrush if necessary. Anytime that you use a piece of furniture for children, make sure that it does not contain lead paint in the finish. If it is more than 10 years old, it is likely to have lead paint. Remove it if necessary.

After cleaning the entire chair, scuff the surface with some sand paper and then wipe it with a tack cloth to remove the dust.

Spray paint was used for this project, but you could use latex. I generally don't use spray paint, but it really is easier for chairs. Choose the color scheme depending on the gender of the child and the room in which it will be placed.

Once the chair is painted in a base color, gather coordinating colors for the freehand designs. Create a different design in various colors on each slat. This step is even easy enough for a child to assist depending on his or her age and ability.

Once the paint has dried thoroughly, coat the decorated sections of the chair in polyurethane for a durable finish.

# $\mathcal{P}$rimitive Plant Stand

Probably one of the most common pieces of furniture found at flea markets is the wooden chair. They can be found in large sets, but more commonly as pairs or alone. But in the end, how many dining chairs does one need? Well, at least one more because a wooden chair can be turned into a charming plant stand for indoor or outdoor use.

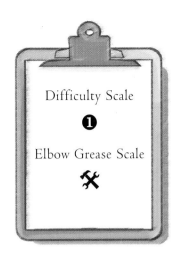

Difficulty Scale

❶

Elbow Grease Scale

**Materials**
detergent
large bowl, basket, pail
  or terra cotta pot
potting soil
flowers

**Tools**
scrub brush
twine/tape
pencil
jigsaw
staple gun and staples
drill and bits

Using laundry detergent (this chair is for the deck so no need to worry about water damage), scrub the chair thoroughly getting the tight spaces with a small brush. Repair any loose joints if needed using wood glue.

Draw guides according to the shape desired for the planter. An easy option is to use a salad bowl, but baskets, pails, terra cotta pots, etc. work just as well. Even chicken wire works when formed into a bowl.

Drill starter holes for the jigsaw blade. Place several around the shape.

Cut the center out of the seat using a jigsaw. Cut about ¼ inch to the inside of the line so that the bowl doesn't fall straight through. A router, hand saw, roto zip, etc. can also be used. Then paint the chair if desired. Paint the newly cut opening in order to resist rot.

Staple the edges of the bowl around the edge of the hole. If the bowl doesn't have a rim, staple around the top on the inside of the cut out. If using chicken wire, turn the chair over and staple the chicken wire to the underside forming a planter area as you go.

Drill holes in the bottom of the bowl for drainage. Choose flowers that will trail over the edges as well as fill in the center.

# $\mathscr{B}$ench

Chairs are one of the easiest furniture items to find. These three chairs were charming, but the one obviously wasn't going to do anyone much good without its legs, but as a bench, they were wonderful. Any three chairs will do. They can be mismatched as far as color or shape, just be sure that the seats are at the same height. Otherwise, you may have to cut down the legs. This bench was perfect for the front porch.

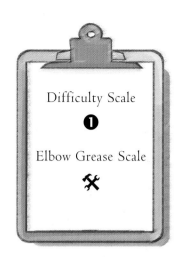

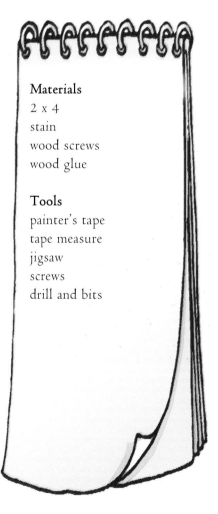

**Materials**
2 x 4
stain
wood screws
wood glue

**Tools**
painter's tape
tape measure
jigsaw
screws
drill and bits

**1**

First, repair any problem with the chairs such as cracks, loose spindles, etc. Use wood glue and painters tape for minor cracks. Use wood glue and binder twine for pulling together loose joints. Remember to clean the areas of debris before applying glue.

Line the chairs up and measure across the bottom to determine the length of your support piece of 2 x 4.

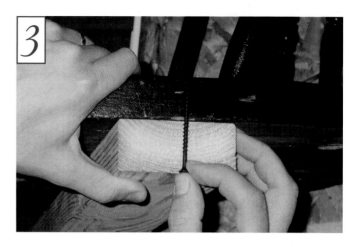

Make sure the screws are long enough to go through the 2 x 4 and into the chair, but not <u>through</u> the seat of the chair.

After making certain the the chairs are evenly spaced, screw the 2 x 4 into the bottom of each chair. Begin with two screws on each end. Then zig-zag those in between.

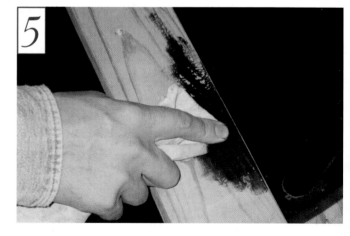

Stain the 2 x 4 to match so that it is less conspicuous. Depending upon the bench, make a custom seat cushion to cover the entire bench or tie single store-bought seat cushions to each individual chair that makes up the bench.

# $\mathcal{H}$ope Chest

This hope chest was a bit outdated with the green stain, but it was very well made. A new finish is all it needed to make a wonderful addition to my master bedroom not only as a blanket chest, but also as a seat at the foot of the bed. A padded seat could easily be added to the top if desired, but I chose to keep it simple.

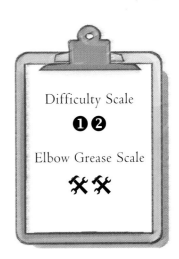

Difficulty Scale
❶ ❷

Elbow Grease Scale
⚒ ⚒

**Materials**
applique
finishing nails
primer
paint
antiquing glaze

**Tools**
screwdriver
hammer
paint brushes/pads
rags

Remove the hardware. This chest had no finish other than the green stain, so it needed a coat of primer. You may only need to scuff the surface of your chest.

Apply a premade wooden applique with wood glue and finishing nails. Hide the nails by placing them in depressions of the applique. Then sink the nail head beyond the surface with a nail set or the point of another nail.

Prime unfinished wood or scuff finished surfaces with sandpaper.

Paint the chest off white.

Brush a thin layer of antiquing glaze into the crevices and onto the applique making sure to get into all the tiny corners.

Rub the antiquing glaze so that it is very thin on flat surfaces or high areas, but leave behind more in the crevices and especially in the applique. Replace hardware once everything has dried.

# Bookcase

This bookcase was nothing special other than it was handmade. It was left behind by a previous tenant when we moved into our first apartment. Books fit well in it and the construction was sturdy so we took it with us when we left. But like I said, there was nothing special about it. So I endeavored to make it special by removing the stickers, adding molding and giving it a nice coat of paint.

Difficulty Scale
❶❷❸

Elbow Grease Scale
⚒ ⚒ ⚒

**Materials**
base molding
crown molding
fluted molding
2 rosettes
finishing nails
paint color of choice
shelving lumber
antiquing glaze
polyurethane

**Tools**
orbital sander
tape measure
wood saw
miter box
hammer
drill and bits
paint brushes/pads
tack cloth
rags

1

Begin by cleaning and removing any unwanted finishes, stickers, nails, etc. Then lightly sand it to get it ready to paint at the end of the project.

Measure along the sides and front edge of the bookcase around the bottom. Using a miter box, cut the base molding to length. Miter the two front corners with a 45° angle much like a picture frame.

Apply the base molding to the bookcase with glue and finishing nails.

Extra pieces of wood may be needed as supports to which you can nail the fluted molding. Screw these into place where needed. We needed them in the 4 outer corners and on the underside of the top shelf.

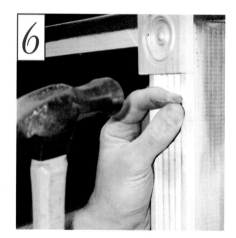

Apply corner rosette molding with construction adhesive and finishing nails.

Measure between each rosette, down the side to the base to determine the length of the fluted molding. Do this between the 2 rosettes as well. Secure with adhesive and finishing nails.

Cut wood shelving 2 inches longer and 1 inch wider than the top. Secure it to the top from the underside of the shelf so the front and sides have a 1-inch overhang. The back should be flush. Fill holes with wood putty and finish.

# Corner Cabinet

I looked high and low for a corner cabinet to fit my oddly laid out half bath. I couldn't find anything that I liked. Everything was too short, too wide, too wicker. Then I found this door. I loved the patina of the old varnish and it had this great little latch on it. I had seen doors made into room divider screens and decided I could make this one into a corner cabinet.

Difficulty Scale
❶ ❷ ❸

Elbow Grease Scale
⚒ ⚒

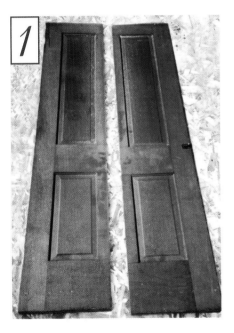

Begin by cutting the door in half lengthwise.

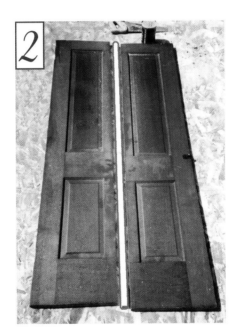

Cut a 1 x 1 piece of lumber to the same length as the door.

**Materials**
1 x 1
shelving
base molding
crown molding
stain
wood screws
finishing nails

**Tools**
drill and bits
screwdrivers
tape measure
carpenter's square
miter box
wood saw
circular saw or table saw
paint brushes/pads
polyurethane

Predrill holes to accommodate screws. Screw the 1 x 1 lumber to the edge of the left half of the door. Turn it on edge and secure the right side of the door to the corresponding side of the 1 x 1 to create a 90° angle.

Measure each side of the "frame" to determine the size of the shelves. The back angle of the shelf is 90° (square.) The front angles are 45°. Screw these into place from the back side of the door frame.

You may need to attach supports for the molding. This is called a nailer. Place them where needed. Here we placed one beneath the bottom shelf to support the base molding.

Use a miter box to cut the base molding to length with a 45° angle on the edges. Nail in place with finishing nails.

The top shelf gets crown molding. Crown molding has 3 surfaces to the back. It should be placed against the top shelf as such. Use a miter box to cut to length. This may take practice so make sure you have enough trim.

Attach the crown molding with finishing nails. Then stain the shelves and molding to match the door as closely as possible or sand and paint the entire piece. Polyurethane any unfinished wood.

# Glossary of Terms

antiqued finish - a finish using a combination of techniques to create a sense of age; includes using historical paint colors and glaze

applique - a decorative trimming sewn, glued, nailed or otherwise attached to a base material

bagged finish - a finish using a scrunched plastic bag to apply paint to create depth and texture

color wheel - a circular graphic showing how colors relate to one another

compound miter saw - a chop saw with a tilting mechanism enabling it to make mitered cuts by rotating the tool's turntable or the head for a bevel cut; a sliding version is available so that it has the ability to move across a span larger than it's own blade; great for molding and trim in addition to many other applications

coping saw - narrow metal frame supporting a very thin blade; makes very fine cuts; makes curved cuts

crackle compound - a glaze-like mixture used to weather or distress a painted finish causing the top coat of paint to crackle as if exposed to the elements over a long period of time

crackle finish - a weathered or distressed finish that mimics the effect of time on a painted surface resulting in crazing and crackling of the paint

denatured alcohol - ethyl alcohol used as a solvent

distressed finish - a finish using a combination of techniques to create a sense of age or exposure to a harsh environment

furniture wax - a paste used for sealing and restoring furniture

glaze - a semitransparent color applied in place of or over a painted surface to modify the effect such as in an antiqued finished; this can be bought in various colors or a colorless version is available that can be tinted using various proportions of latex painted depending upon the desire effect

grout - a thin mortar used to fill the spaces between tiles

grout float - a tool used to apply grout having a rubber pad that glides over the top of a tiled surface without pulling the grout out of the spaces between

latex paint - water-based paint that is easily cleaned up with water and soap; drying time is much less than oil-based paints; little to no odor that is nontoxic

lead-based paint - paint once commonly used before 1973 that contained lead; now known to be harmful is handled frequently or if loose paint chips are ingested; long-term exposure is known to cause health problems including brain damage; should be stripped from furniture especially if it will be accessible to children

miter - to cut on an angle to form a corner as in a picture frame

molding - ornamental trim often placed around a room where the floor meets the wall or where the ceiling meets the wall; also used for finishing doorways, windows and furniture

mortise - in a joint, the notch or hole in which a corresponding tenon in inserted

mosaic - created by inlaying small bits of tile, glass, stone, etc. to produce an overall design or picture

nail set - used to sink a nail beneath the surface of the wood without damaging the surrounding area

oil-based paint - solvent-based paint made from a mixture of resins and oils that must be cleaned up with turpentine; the drying time is lengthy; has a noxious odor; is very durable and can even be used for floors; has a beautiful satin look

polyurethane - used as a sealer to protect wood furniture; used in the same manner that varnish was once used to create a durable finish

primer - a preliminary coat of paint that prepares a surface for painting by acting as a key to provide better adhesion between the item and the top coat of finish paint; is recommended for drywall, wood, metal, etc.; helps cover stains and previous paint colors from showing through the final coat of paint; protects metals from rusting

quick-action clamps - designed for quick and easy operation, a lower jaw slides back and forth on a bar and locks securely in place to create pressure where needed

router - power tool with various bits that can create intricate designs, decorative edges, carving and cut cabinet joints

shellac - a thin, usually clear varnish made from lac (a resin) and alcohol

sponge finish - a finish utilizing various shades of paint and a sea sponge to create depth and texture

stain - a pigment applied to the surface of wood to color it without obscuring the grain

stenciling - creating a pattern or design by using a thin plastic or paper cutout so that the paint appears on the surface beneath in the shape of the void

stripping paint - to remove the paint from a surface by using a solvent

tack cloth - a resin coated cloth which attracts dust and leaves the surface cleaner even than a vacuum or air gun

tenon - the protruding part of a joint made to fit into a corresponding mortise or hole

thin set - the mortar used to adhere tile to a surface such as a floor, backsplash or tabletop

trowel - a tool used to scoop, spread or smooth thin set or cement as in tiling or bricklaying; generally has a thin flat triangular blade

twine - strong cord made up of two more more strand twisted together; often used to bind

veneer - a thin layer of a more costly material adhered to a less costly base material as with a fine wood layer covering a more common wood; a superficial layer primarily to enhance the appearance

woodworm - not actually a worm, these are the larvae of several types of beetles; the eggs are laid and once hatched, the larvae tunnel through the wood until they exit as adults leaving behind holes that compromise the structural integrity of the wood; these species of woodboring insects are repelled by some types of wood one of which is mahogany from Central America used a great deal in Victorian furniture

# Index